The Character Club

The Character Club

"It's time to POWER UP!"

Written by: **Joshua P. Cole, Ph.D.**   Illustrated by: **Scott M. Nista**

Copyright © 2017 by A New Angle: Creating Equity in Education
The Character Club artwork (Copyright © 2016) are creations of author, Joshua P. Cole and illustrator Scott M. Nista per the Copyright Office of the United States Register of Copyrights and Director: VAu 1-240-669

All rights reserved. This book or any portion thereof may not be reproduced or transmitted in any form by any means, including photocopying, recording, or other electronic or mechanical methods, without the prior written permission of the publisher, except in the case of brief quotations embodied in critical reviews and certain other noncommercial uses permitted by copyright law. For permission requests, write to the publisher at joshuapcole@gmail.com
Printed in the United States of America
First Printing, 2017
ISBN 978-0-692-79100-4
LCCN 2016918014
To learn more about *A NEW Angle* and to access resources for "The Character Club" **visit:**
www.joshuapcole.com

This book is dedicated to all of the superhero teachers, staff, parents and students at Ecoff Elementary School.

Table of Contents

Chapter 1: A Mystery at Hillview — Page 1

Chapter 2: Sebastian — Page 5

Chapter 3: Grace — Page 8

Chapter 4: Carissa — Page 11

Chapter 5: Santiago — Page 14

Chapter 6: Oki — Page 17

Chapter 7: Zoe — Page 20

Chapter 8: Guyton — Page 23

Chapter 9: A Clue — Page 26

Chapter 10: Teamwork — Page 29

Chapter 11: POWER UP! — Page 33

Chapter 1
A Mystery at Hillview

Like other schools, Hillview Elementary is home to students who have great powers. All students have the ability to be their very best, but some students have lost the powers that make them strong inside. Such powers should be found in their hearts and minds. These powers give students inner character strengths and the ability to be proud of who they are as a person.

Some students stopped believing in themselves and gave up on their goals. The students at Hillview needed help to become their very best again. Their teachers, families, and friends tried to help, but nothing worked until something very special happened…

One night, out of a cloudless sky, a powerful thunderstorm began right above Hillview Elementary School. **ZZZAP!**

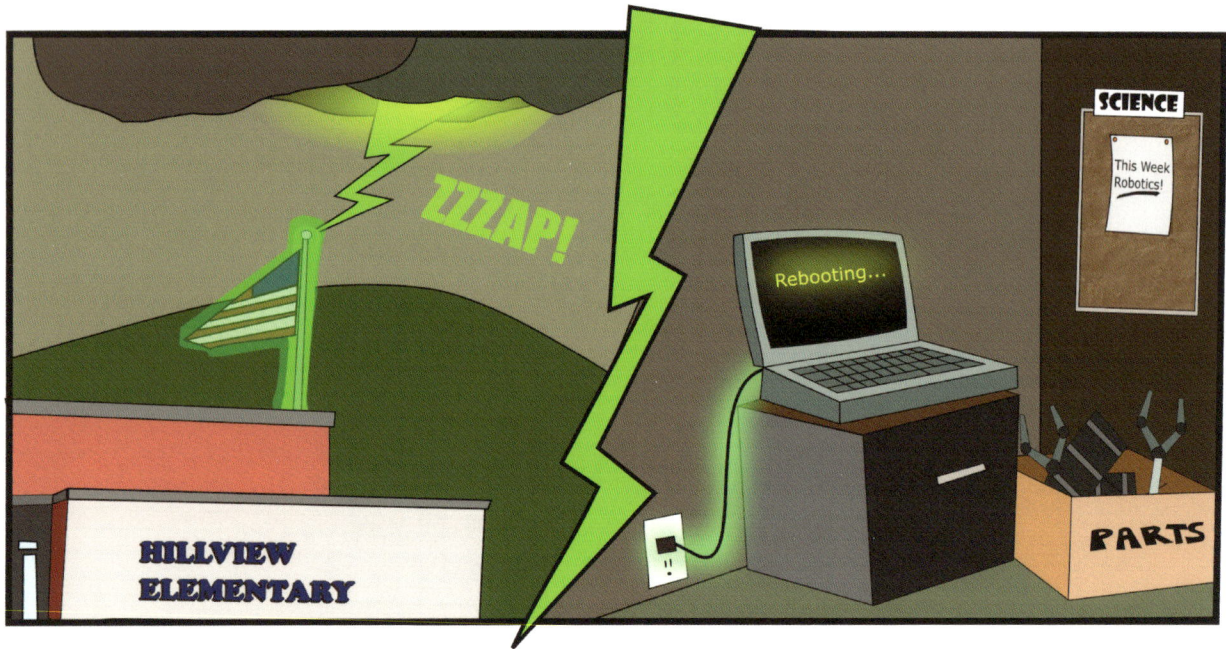

Lightning struck Hillview, and the electricity from that bolt traveled all the way to a laptop computer in the school's storage room. The screen popped open and lit up as bright as the lightning that brought it to life! The jolt of electricity disconnected the computer from the wall outlet, and it fell into a box of parts. A few seconds later, the computer had arms, wheels, and a face! Then it began to talk!

"Hello, my name is **Query**. How may I help empower you?"

Zoom-ziggity-ziggity-zoom! Query had a blast scooting around the school all night long. This regular laptop had transformed into a super computer with superpowers!

The next day, when no one was looking, Query quickly transformed back into a laptop computer. None of the students, teachers, custodians, or even the principal knew Query existed.

Looking like a regular computer, Query secretly listened to everyone talking and found out that many kids were not living up to their full potential. Query could tell many students needed help finding their abilities to become powerful again. Query made a list of seven inner characters strengths the students needed to find.

1. Self-control to be aware of their choices and interactions with others.
2. Gratitude to be thankful for what they have in life.
3. Curiosity to learn new things in life.
4. Social intelligence to come up with ideas to get along with others.
5. Optimism to be hopeful about their future.
6. Zest to have a positive energy in life.
7. Grit to stay motivated to reach their goals.

Query came up with a plan that would empower seven special students to find the powers they had lost. Query knew that these seven students had the potential to be great leaders. What Query did next would soon become a mystery at Hillview Elementary School.

Chapter 2
Sebastian

Sebastian used to make good choices. However, he began making bad choices and getting himself into trouble. He would blurt out in class, and could not keep his hands and feet to himself. To help him make better choices, he had a goal to build mechanical arms in his backpack that would pop out with the push of a button. He wanted to program the hands to help him from talking too much, and to grab his arms and feet when he was not being responsible.

He also wanted his mechanical arms to guide him outside to exercise instead of staying inside and playing video games. He needed help grabbing healthy snacks rather than junk food, too. However, he never began building the arms because he was unable to focus.

Whenever anyone tried to help him stay focused, he would become very angry. Even when he tried to listen, he would interrupt before the other person could finish. Sebastian came across as being rude. He had lost his self-control over his actions and interactions with others.

One day, Sebastian couldn't find his backpack to pack up to go home from school. He went to the art room to look for his backpack and found it on a windowsill. Since he didn't pay attention very well, he didn't notice that his backpack was glowing. Sebastian spun around quickly and slid his backpack onto his shoulders. All of a sudden, Sebastian felt a burst of positive energy flowing through his entire body. **BOOM!** For the first time in a long time, he felt a sense of awareness about himself and his ability to be responsible. He knew something special had happened to his backpack, and he wanted to use his new power to make good choices.

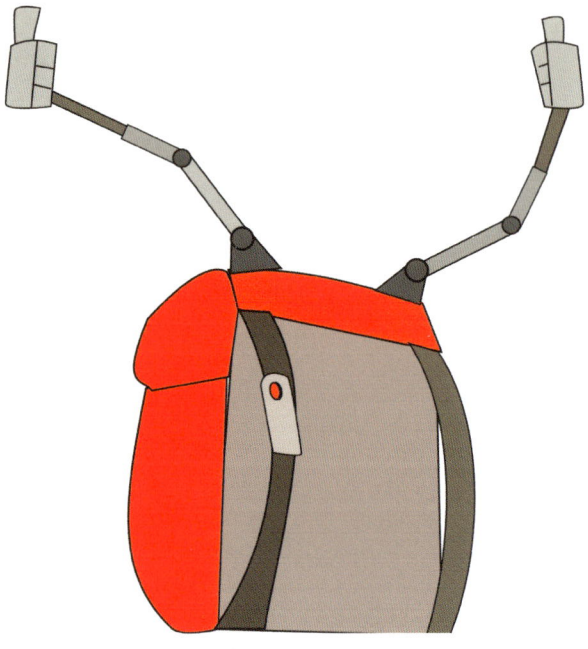

What happened next was outstanding! Sebastian calmly made his way to the bus, sat quietly in his seat, and came up with a plan for the rest of the day. The plan included finishing his goal of building mechanical arms for his backpack. When he got home, he ate a healthy snack, finished his chores, completed his homework, rode his bike to get some exercise, and built the mechanical arms for his backpack.

Sebastian put his backpack on, clicked the button on the strap to activate the mechanical arms, and heard, *"Chee-choo-choo-choo-choo-chuh."* He looked over his shoulders to see his mechanical arms come to life! He pushed the button again and with a *"Chee-choo-choo-choo-choo-chuh,"* the arms went back into his backpack. He thought, *Now I can use these arms to help me make good choices*. Sebastian had never felt more focused in his entire life.

While brushing his teeth before bed, Sebastian could tell he was becoming more aware of his choices. His backpack had given him the power to be in control of himself, but he still wondered how this had happened. Sebastian made a plan to keep his special backpack and mechanical arms a secret while he worked to solve the mystery of how his backpack gave him the superpower of self-control.

Chapter 3

Grace

Grace used to show appreciation to her family and pets. She used to love playing soccer and learning about science too. Deep down inside, she was a very kind-hearted and caring person. Unfortunately, her parents didn't get along very well and this made her sad. In time, they separated and eventually got a divorce. Grace went between her parents' houses and ended up staying with her grandmother a lot. During this time, she would get mad very easily. She began to lose appreciation for the things she had in life. Instead of being grateful for what she did have, she focused on what she didn't have. She didn't care about her family, her pets, soccer, or science anymore.

The only time Grace would say "thank you" to someone was when she was forced to. She had lost her sense of gratefulness toward others and for what life had to offer. Even when her grandmother gave her a dreamcatcher pouch with a beautiful heart woven into it, she refused to show any gratitude. Grace took the pouch to school, hung it in the back of her locker, and never used it.

One day, the girl whose locker was next to Grace's said, "I thought you'd like to have these really cool pencils," and placed them in Grace's hands. The girl walked away, and Grace rolled her eyes as if to say, *I don't want your silly pencils.* Grace looked for a trashcan, but couldn't find one. Then she remembered the pouch in the back of her locker. When Grace opened the flap on the pouch to toss in the pencils, she froze. All of a sudden, she felt a rush of positive energy throughout her body that went directly to her heart. **SHHOO!** She quickly stuffed the pencils inside, and noticed the pouch was glowing.

Grace put the pouch around her shoulder and felt the ability to be thankful again, which she hadn't felt in a long time. She knew something very special had happened to her pouch and wanted to use her new power to show appreciation to people in her life again.

What happened next was wonderful! Grace found the girl who'd given her the pencils and thanked her. She went around Hillview thanking others who had done nice things for her, including her teacher for teaching her. Most importantly, as soon as Grace got home, she gave her grandmother a giant hug for the dreamcatcher pouch, and for her love and support. Grace then called both of her parents and told them that she loved them very much. Next, she went outside for the first time in a long while to play soccer. She also began playing with her pets and reading her science books again.

Grace went to bed that night, thankful for her life as she snuggled her pets. She was becoming happier and grateful again. Still, she couldn't help but wonder how her pouch had become so powerful. She wanted to keep her special pouch a secret until she could uncover the mystery of how it gave her the superpower of gratitude.

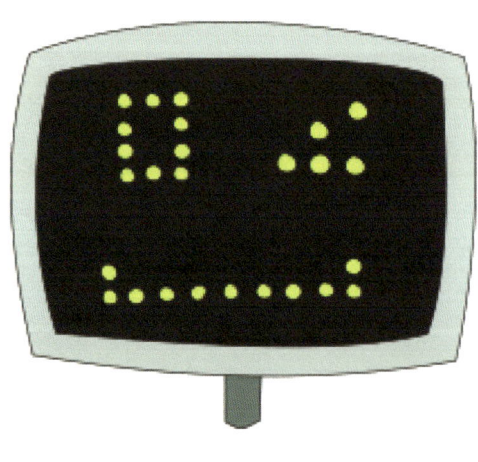

Chapter 4

Carissa

Carissa used to be the best student at Hillview. Her favorite subjects were writing and social studies. She used to love learning new things and thinking about creative ideas. However, she stopped asking questions in school because she started to be teased for being smart. Things got even worse after she got glasses. She didn't like wearing her glasses because some kids would call her names. Her feelings were hurt. Carissa stopped being who she truly was so others would like her.

Carissa hid her glasses in her desk so she wouldn't be picked on. She was becoming unsure of herself. She wanted to be liked by others, so she stopped showing how smart she was. Carissa's interest in exploring new ideas went away, and she no longer asked questions to learn new things in school.

One day, Carissa reached into her desk for a pencil. Her pinky finger slightly touched her glasses. She felt a vibration of positive energy flow from her pinky, through her hand, up her arm, and rumble throughout her body like a drumroll. **BADUM!** She slid down in her seat, peeked into her desk, and saw a glow coming from her glasses. Carissa couldn't tell if the light was just a reflection off her lenses or if there was another reason for this odd situation. For the first time in a long time, she began to wonder. She wanted to learn what had happened to her glasses. She did what any curious student would do. She decided to put on her glasses.

The vibration she felt before increased one hundred times. **BADUM! BADUM! BADUM!** Carissa felt a sense of confidence in her ability to ask questions again so she could learn more. She decided to use her new power to explore and learn new things.

What happened next was fantastic! Carissa began asking her teacher questions. She was also eager to use a computer to start researching new things. Before going home that day, she went to the library to check out several books to read. Carissa walked around, wearing her glasses with her new sense of confidence. Some students were still mean and teased her about her glasses. However, Carissa felt stronger within her heart and mind about herself. She wasn't as upset by any of the students who still picked on her. Instead, she focused on being who she truly was.

That night, Carissa finished reading one of her new books and wrote about what she had learned in her journal. Carissa was thinking and feeling like her old self again. She thought, *How could I help others feel stronger inside too, especially those who still tease me?* She fell asleep knowing that she would keep her special glasses a secret. Carissa was determined to solve the mystery of how they gave her the superpower of curiosity.

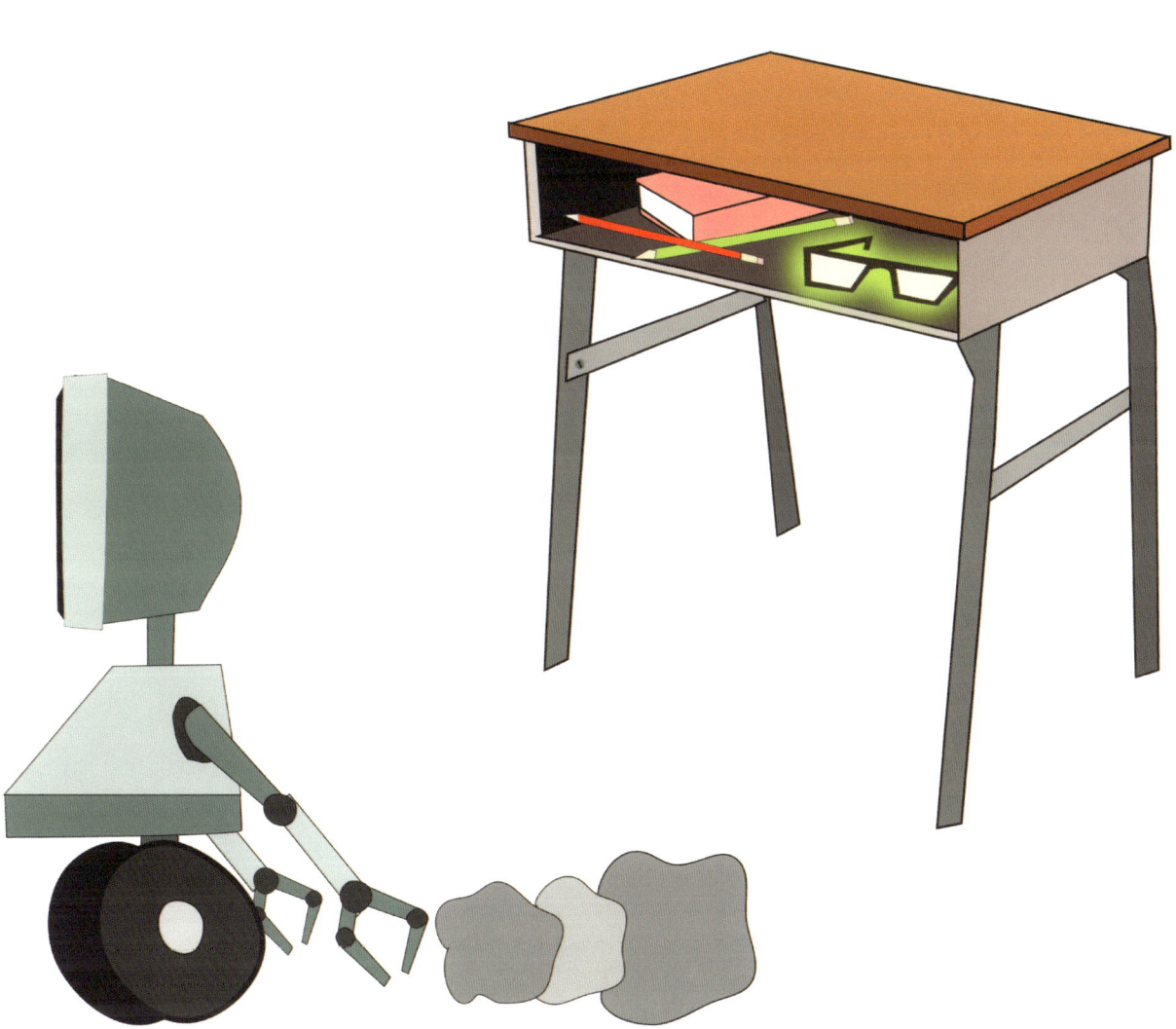

Chapter 5

Santiago

Santiago used to be a good friend and football teammate at school. However, yelling and fighting began to happen more often in his home and neighborhood. This made Santiago angry. He started having trouble finding solutions to problems with others. Sometimes he would get mad because he couldn't understand why other people would become frustrated with him.

Santiago had a very hard time working through his problems and didn't really seem to care what other people were thinking or feeling. He had difficulties at Hillview with his friends, at home with his family and neighbors, and on the field with his football teammates. His disagreements with others would often go from bad to worse because he never cared to understand their points of view. Santiago had lost his empathy, which is the ability to care about other people's feelings.

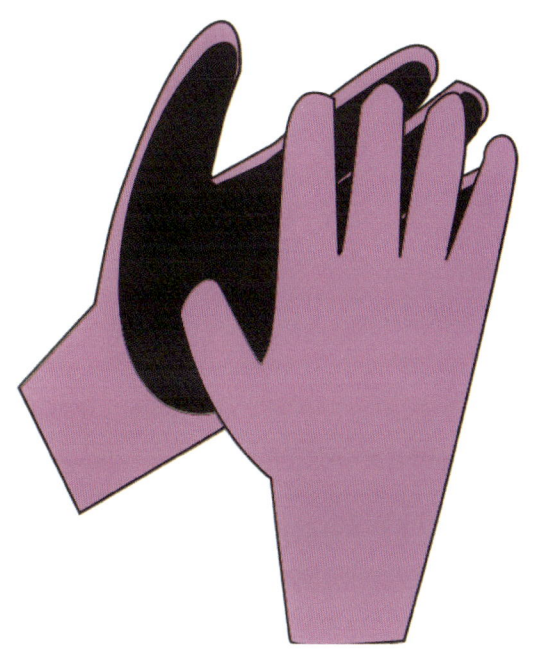

One day during recess, he couldn't find his football gloves, and nobody wanted to help him because they were tired of his bad attitude. Santiago went alone to the Lost and Found to see if he could find them. Santiago spotted his gloves sticking out of the box of lost items. He bent down to pick them up and noticed they looked a little strange. The gloves appeared to be glowing and were giving off a positive energy that gave him a sense of peace and happiness. When he slid the first glove on, a shockwave of joy burst through his body and went straight to his heart. **WHAM!** He suddenly regained an awareness for finding solutions to problems he was having with others. He slid on the other glove. **WHAM!** The feeling that he hadn't felt in a long time happened again. This time it went directly to his brain. He felt a sense of awareness about his ability to think of ideas to get along with others. Santiago knew something special had happened to his gloves, so he decided to use his new power to work on the problems he'd been having with other people.

What happened next was amazing! For the rest of the day, Santiago worked on developing solutions to the difficulties he was having with his classmates, family members, neighbors, and football teammates. When he gave a hug, handshake, or high five, all of a sudden, a rush of positive thoughts and feelings would come over him about the person he used to disrespect. His viewpoint of others had changed, and he was coming up with bright ideas to deal with all types of problems. He suddenly began to understand other people's points of view about difficulties he once had with them. Santiago was becoming much better at getting along with others. He made up his mind that from then on, he would talk to others about how he felt. More importantly, he told himself, *I will listen when they share their feelings with me.*

After a day of thinking of ideas to solve problems, Santiago was feeling better inside. However, he went to sleep still wondering how his gloves became so powerful and decided to keep them a secret. He began to think of ideas to solve the mystery of how his gloves gave him the superpower of social intelligence.

Chapter 6
Oki

Oki was a new student to Hillview from Japan. At her last school, she used to be involved in school plays. She used to love music and putting on shows with her friends. However, moving to a new place had been difficult for her. She had to learn English and make new friends at the same time. Oki felt that her life was terrible. She failed all the tests she took and wasn't very hopeful that things would get any better.

Oki was becoming quite a pessimist because she worried that things would keep getting worse. She also quit trying to study or make friends. In fact, she stayed inside, by herself, during recess every day. She walked around school wearing an old gray coat with her head hung low. Oki couldn't see any way to improve her life because she had lost her ability to be hopeful.

One day, when heading back to class after sitting alone in the library, Oki remembered she'd left her coat on a chair. She moaned and groaned back to the library. As she moped along, she worried about what else might go wrong. When she saw her coat, it was inside out, and the bright yellow side was showing. *Oh no; what now?* she thought. When she reached for the coat, she noticed it had a glow to it, which was very different from its usual gloomy gray appearance. She took the coat by the collar, spun it around her head, and put her arms into the sleeves. Suddenly, a positive energy began to travel throughout her entire body. **WHOOSH!** She felt a sense of hope that she hadn't felt in a long time. It was as if she found her ability to be hopeful again. She thought, *If I put forth enough effort, I could shape my life to be positive*. Oki knew something special had happened to her coat, and she wanted to use her new power to find ways to improve how things were going at her new school.

What happened next was incredible! Oki went back to class with her new positive outlook, hoping she would have a great rest of her day. Even when things didn't go well, Oki stayed motivated and felt she could learn lessons when difficult things happened to her. She took another test and still didn't pass. Oki was upset, but this time, she didn't give up. She decided that she would need to study more instead of feeling like she was a failure. She also tried talking to other students. When they didn't want to talk to her, she thought, *Maybe they're just having a bad day*. Oki decided that every day, she would make an effort to make new friendships by playing at recess, and she would even join the Drama Club. She was also excited to learn English.

During dinner with her family, Oki practiced her English and shared she was going to be more hopeful about her future, which meant she was becoming more optimistic again (the opposite of pessimistic). She couldn't help but wonder how her coat reversed her thinking about life. She came up with a strategy to keep her special coat a secret while she worked on solving the mystery of how it gave her the superpower of optimism.

Chapter 7
Zoe

Zoe used to be happy and had many friends. Others thought she was cool because of her cool clothes. However, Zoe's life changed suddenly when her dad lost his job, her mom became very sick, and they had to sell their house. Her family could no longer afford many things. They also had to sell many of her clothes, and Zoe was only able to keep one pair of shoes. Soon, girls who she thought were her friends were teasing her. Zoe became very sad and shy; she felt misunderstood.

There were many activities for her to participate in at school, but Zoe no longer cared to do things that involved being around other people. She wanted to be liked by others for who she truly was, but on the inside, she felt very lonely.

One day, Zoe went to the nurse's office because she had blisters on the heels of her feet. The nurse told Zoe to take off her shoes and rest. Zoe took a nap while the nurse was busy at her desk. When Zoe woke up, she saw her shoes glowing under a bench. Zoe thought, *Am I dreaming?* She rubbed her eyes and slipped her feet into her shoes. Just then, sparks of positive energy rushed through her body like a flash of lightning. **ZING! ZING!** Zoe felt a sense of excitement for life that she hadn't felt in a long time. She smiled as she used her ability to replace negative feelings with a positive energy. Zoe knew something special had happened to her shoes, and she had the desire to use her new power to brighten up her life and to cheer up others.

What happened next was fabulous! Zoe used her newfound energy to deal with the challenges in her life with a positive mindset. She worked hard to stay happy about life even though everything wasn't perfect. She didn't change who she was as a person to please other people, and that is what made her special. Instead, she focused on what she was interested in doing…and did it. One thing she had never shared with anyone was her interest in learning chess. She asked her teacher how to sign up for the Chess Club, and then went to practice after school. Others noticed this change in Zoe and were impressed by her positive attitude. Zoe was starting to smile again and didn't let the mean students bother her anymore. People could tell that Zoe's happiness had increased, and it was positively influencing others.

Zoe went home after chess practice and was feeling excited about life again. She had her energy back! Zoe and her dad called her mom in the hospital and encouraged her to get well soon. This helped her family stay positive. Zoe kept her special shoes a secret while she thought of plan to find out what had happened to them. She was so excited to solve the mystery of how her shoes gave her the superpower of zest.

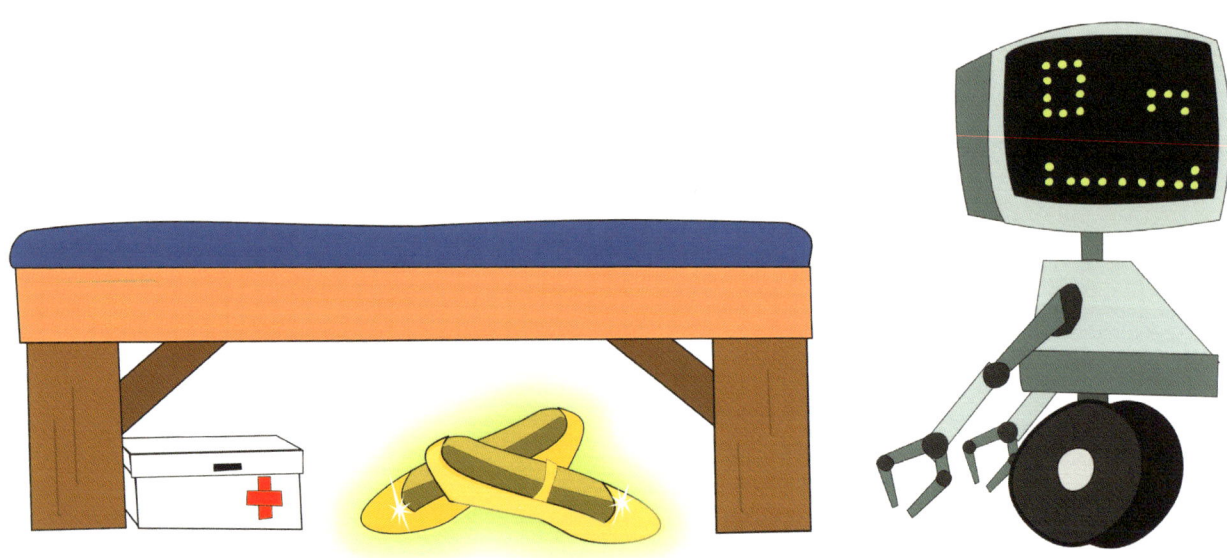

Chapter 8
Guyton

Guyton used to have an inner strength that allowed him to work hard to become the best math student at Hillview. He also used to be the fastest runner on the track team. However, as he grew older, he developed a medical condition in his legs, and in time, he was unable to walk. Guyton began using a wheelchair to get around. This made Guyton feel powerless.

He tried to compete in wheelchair races, but it was difficult because his hands would get sweaty. His coach gave him wristbands to help, but Guyton got frustrated and didn't want to use them. Guyton chose to quit the track team. He also gave up on his math work. He put his wristbands and math supplies in his pencil box and stuffed the box into the back pocket of his wheelchair. Guyton lost his motivation to be the best he could be at track and math. Guyton felt that he had lost his passion and purpose in life.

One day, Guyton bumped into a drinking fountain in the hallway, and his pencil box flew out of his wheelchair. The box popped open, and the stuff inside went everywhere. Guyton thought to himself, *Oh man, life just keeps getting worse for me.* He began picking up the mess he made and saw that his wristbands had slid down the hallway by the computer lab. He wheeled himself towards the wristbands and noticed they were glowing. Guyton thought this was very unusual. As he reached down to pick them up, a rush of energy traveled through his body. He slipped the first wristband on and **VOOM!** Then the second, **VOOM! VOOM!** He felt a sense of motivation that he hadn't felt in a long time. He wanted to use his ability to refocus on his goals in track and math. Guyton knew something special had happened to his wristbands, and he decided to use his new power to restore the passion and purpose in his life.

What happened next was awesome! Guyton went back to class and began working on math again. He loved math so much and wasn't going to let anything stop him from doing what he enjoyed. Guyton didn't do very well on the next math test he took, but he was determined to learn from his mistakes. He also went to his track coach and asked if he could rejoin the track team to compete in the upcoming wheelchair races. Guyton knew it was his responsibility to work hard at math and to compete in track no matter how difficult the challenge.

Guyton was getting back to his old self, of being motivated to reach his goals. He went to sleep that night determined to be successful in school, track, and life. He knew that it wouldn't be easy and that he might fail at times; however, he was always going to put forth his very best effort. Guyton decided to keep his special wristbands a secret as he worked to solve the mystery of how they gave him the superpower of grit.

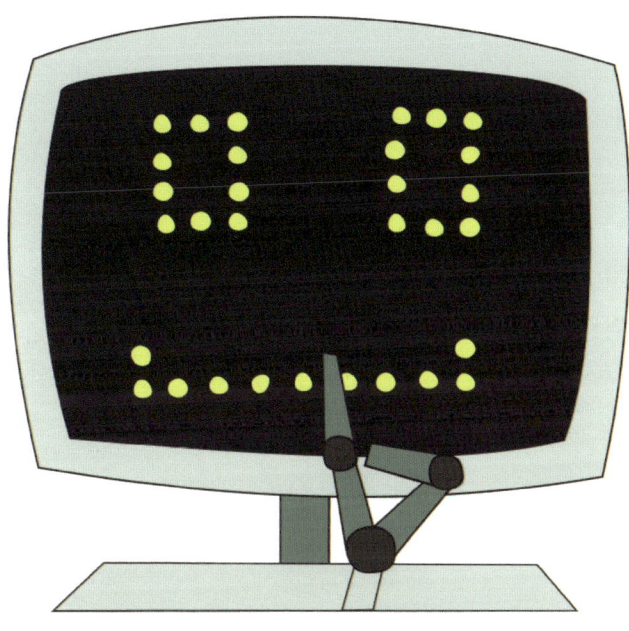

Chapter 9

A Clue

Several weeks had passed and all seven of the students were still keeping their powers and special belongings a secret. The seven students wanted to know how their backpack, pouch, glasses, gloves, coat, shoes, and wristbands gave them the superpowers of **self-control**, **gratitude, curiosity, social intelligence**, **optimism**, **zest,** and **grit**. They didn't realize it, but their powers were getting stronger every day.

Each student was in a different class at Hillview, so they never crossed paths while searching for clues. They just snuck around the school trying to solve the mystery of how they got their powers. This mystery went unsolved until they each separately received a clue!

Throughout one day at school, during each of their own computer classes, the seven students received an interesting message on the laptop computer they were using. The message flashed:

> **I have been watching you use your powers. Meet in Room 701 after school today at 4 o'clock!**

Each of them thought, *Wow, I wonder who wrote this message?* At 4 o'clock, all of the students reported to Room 701, which was a storage room at Hillview. They were eager to solve their own mysteries. When they arrived, they were confused as to why there were six other students in the room. Suddenly, they saw something scoot out from behind some boxes. **ZOOM-ZIG-ZAG-ZOOM!** Everyone stared in complete shock as a super computer was *zigging, zagging,* and *zooming* around the room. Suddenly it stopped and said, "Hello! Welcome to the Empowerment Room. My name is Query and I have empowered all of you with inner character strengths to become superheroes." All of the students' jaws dropped as Query explained that they were empowered to be leaders at Hillview. The students continued to stand in silence until Query asked them, "Would all of you like to become official superheroes of the Character Club?" All seven students cheered!

Then one by one, Query took their superhero shirts out from a box labeled "TOP SECRET." Each shirt had a symbol on it to represent each superhero's superpower.

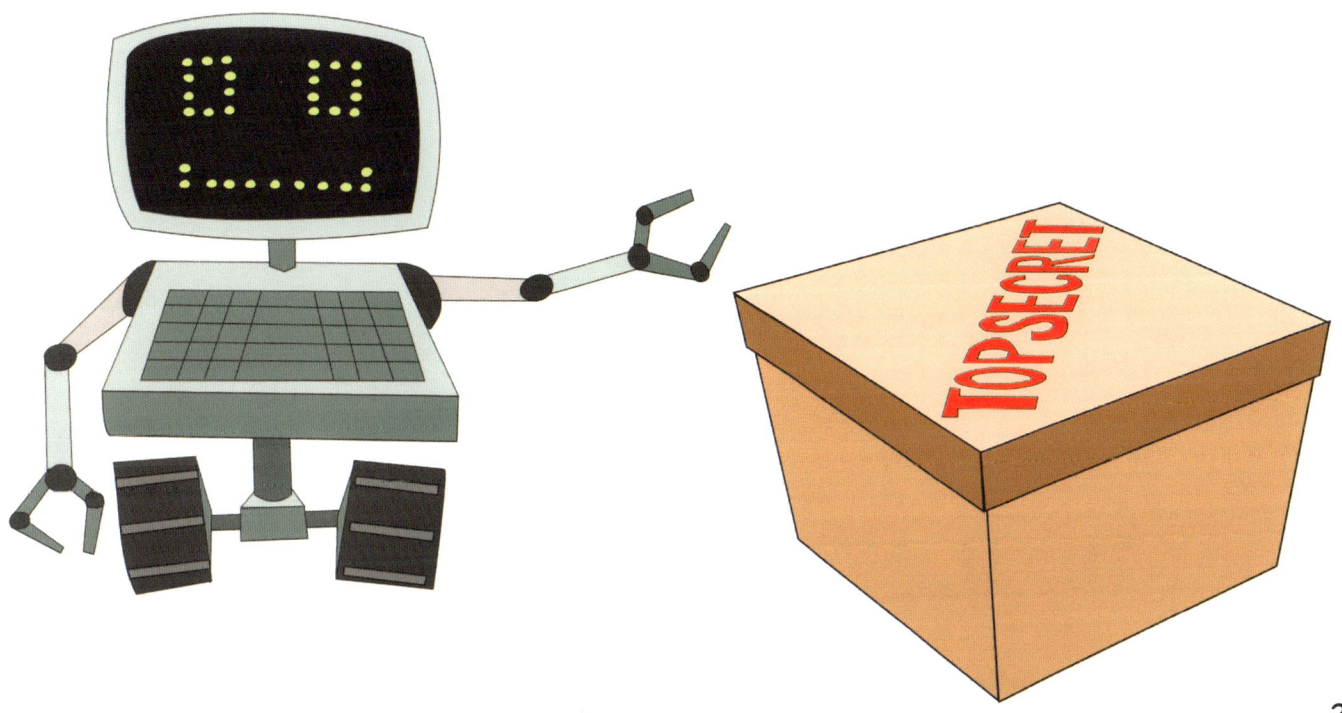

*Sebastian's symbol was an **eye** for his power of self-control to be aware of his choices and interactions with others.*

*Grace's symbol was a **heart** for her power of gratitude to be thankful.*

*Carissa's symbol was a **question mark** for her power of curiosity to learn new things.*

*Santiago's symbol was a **lightning bolt** for his power of social intelligence for coming up with ideas to get along with others.*

*Oki's symbol was a **smiley face** for her power of optimism to be hopeful about her future.*

*Zoe's symbol was a **spark** for her power of zest to have a positive energy in life.*

*Guyton's symbol was an **exclamation point** for his power of grit to stay motivated to reach his goals.*

All of the students smiled with pride as Query introduced the team and gave them their superhero shirts. Then, Query's screen turned into their team symbol. It was a power sign with an arrow pointing up to the sky. Query said, "Welcome to the Character Club. It's time to POWER UP!"

Chapter 10
Teamwork

Sebastian is now focused on making good choices and developing positive relationships with others. He is living healthy, aware of what he says, paying attention more, and making new inventions. If he gets angry about anything, he is able to stay calm and make good choices without always relying on his mechanical arms for help. Sebastian will use his power of awareness to be a leader, and empower others with the ability to manage their choices, under his superhero name of **Self-Control!**

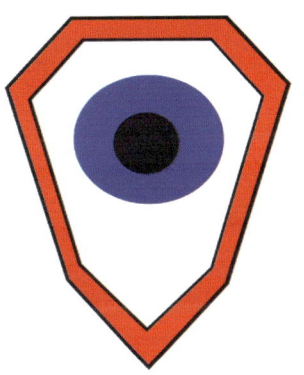

Grace now says "thank you" in response to nice things people say or do for her. She also does nice things for others whom she appreciates in her life. Her pouch became the storage place for the special gifts she gives to people and her pets. She is also studying more science and playing more soccer. Grace will use her power of thankfulness to be a leader, and empower others with the ability to appreciate all they have in life, under her superhero name of **Gratitude!**

Carissa is now reading more books, asking more questions, and trying new things like writing stories in her journal. She has become an even better student in social studies, is making good friendships, and has become more confident. Carissa's mind is more active and open to a whole new world of knowledge. Carissa will use her power of learning to be a leader, and empower others with the ability to learn more, under her superhero name of **Curiosity**!

Santiago is now able to adapt to all types of social situations and comes up with intellectual ideas to handle problems with a positive attitude. He is able to get along better with his friends, family, neighbors, and football teammates. He also uses empathy to help him understand how others feel. Santiago will use his power of coming up with ideas to solve conflicts to be a leader, and empower others with the ability to get along with each other, under his superhero name of **Social Intelligence**!

Oki is now becoming very hopeful and active in her life. She is doing a great job learning English and has become very involved with the Drama Club. Oki has faced her challenges with the support of her new friends and family. Her mood has changed to be positive, and she is now happy at Hillview. Oki will use her power of hope to be a leader, and empower others with the ability to stay positive and happy in their lives despite the difficulties they may face, under her superhero name of **Optimism!**

Zoe is now able to be the person she truly is inside without worrying about what other people think of her. She has a positive outlook on life and uses her happy spirit to support others. Zoe has also become the captain of the Chess Club. She remains excited about all the good that life has to offer, even though her family is still going through some difficult situations. Zoe will use her power of positive energy to be a leader, and empower others with the ability to stay excited about life, under her superhero name of **Zest**!

 **Guyton** is now motivated to accomplish all of his goals. He has become a leader on the track team, even though he hasn't won any medals in his wheelchair races yet. Guyton is also working hard at his math skills and trying his best even when he fails. He is committed to the passion that is in his heart and is making a positive impact on others. Guyton will use his power of motivation to reach his goals to be a leader, and empower others with the ability to discover their inner strengths, under his superhero name of **Grit**!

Query told the superheroes, "All seven of you will need to work together as a team to empower other students at Hillview." The superheroes looked at each other and thought the same thing: *By working together, we can learn new powers from our teammates and help other students be powerful too.* The Character Club was excited to use teamwork to empower each other and the other students at Hillview!

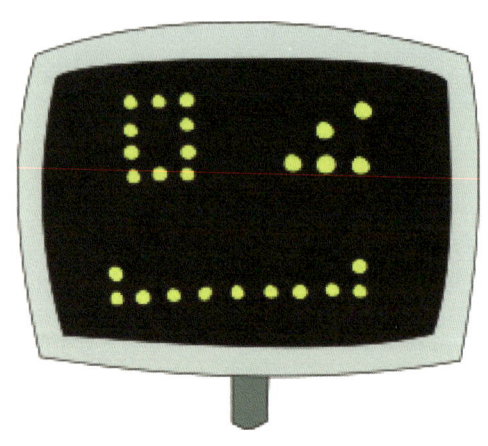

Chapter 11
POWER UP!

Query told the Character Club, "I have one more surprise for you." ***Zoom-ziggity-ziggity-zoom!*** In a flash, Query scooted to the other side of the room and back. This time, Query was carrying a small box labeled "TOP TOP SECRET."

Query reached in and pulled out an electronic device that looked like a video game controller. Query called it the Power Pod!

The Power Pod had seven buttons that matched the seven symbols on each of the seven superheroes' shirts. Query explained that when a member of the Character Club was needed, their button would be pushed on the Power Pod. Then, the symbol on their shirt would light up as a signal for them to report to the Empowerment Room and receive their secret missions. Room 701 was a storage room for the rest of the school, but for the Character Club, it became their Secret Mission Control Center!

Query asked if anyone had any questions, and not surprisingly, the superheroes were all still wondering the same thing: *How did Query empower us?* Curiosity asked the question: "How did you make our belongings give us our superpowers?" Query smiled and said, "Your glasses, Sebastian's backpack, Carissa's pouch, Santiago's gloves, Oki's coat, Zoe's shoes, or even Guyton's wristbands didn't give each of you your superpowers; you always had these powers inside of you. Each of you just needed a reminder that you never lost your abilities." Query went on to say,

"When you have a growth mindset, you can give the extra effort to make your inner character strengths and abilities stronger. Also, with a positive attitude, you can accomplish all of your goals to make the world a better place."

At that moment, the Character Club understood their purpose was to help empower other students to reach their full potentials in life. As superheroes, they would use their superpowers to help other students improve their inner character strengths.

From that day forward, Query contacted the Character Club with the Power Pod when other students needed help with their self-control, gratitude, curiosity, social intelligence, optimism, zest, or grit.

The superheroes would meet in the Empowerment Room and use teamwork to come up with creative ideas to empower other students. Before heading out on their missions, Query would say, "It's time to" and the Character Club would put their fists together and say…

"POWER UP!"

The Character Club now empowers students at Hillview to be their very best. The superheroes build trust and respect with other students by being kind and listening to their needs. They support everyone's personal growth, even if it takes a long time to improve their inner character strengths. The hearts and minds of all students at Hillview are becoming stronger because they are using their powers to be a team. Thanks to the Character Club, Hillview Elementary is now the best school in the world!

Acknowledgments

My wife, Heather, for your endless support; you are my blessing in life.

My son, Silas, whom I aspire to inspire.

-J.C.

My wife, Jennifer, and children Jacob, Samantha, and Jackson.

They make me feel like the luckiest husband and dad in the world.

-S.N.

CPSIA information can be obtained at www.ICGtesting.com
Printed in the USA
BVIW12n0825300617
488222BV00005B/23